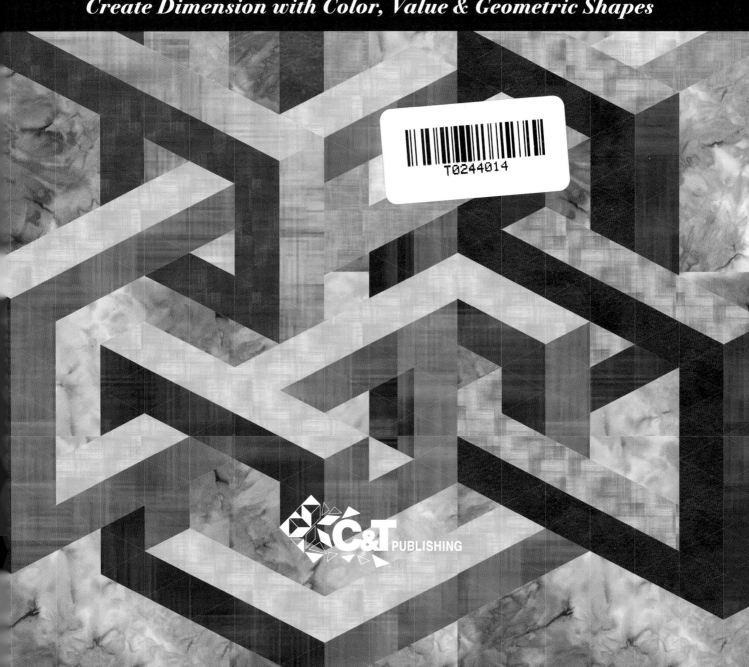

Ruth Ann Berry

Stunning
3-D Quilts Simplified

Create Dimension with Color, Value & Geometric Shapes

C&T PUBLISHING

Text and photography copyright © 2020 by Ruth Ann Berry
Photography and artwork copyright © 2020 by C&T Publishing, Inc.

PUBLISHER: Amy Barrett-Daffin
CREATIVE DIRECTOR: Gailen Runge
ACQUISITIONS EDITOR: Roxane Cerda
MANAGING EDITOR: Liz Aneloski
EDITOR: Karla Menaugh
TECHNICAL EDITOR: Del Walker
COVER/BOOK DESIGNER: April Mostek
PRODUCTION COORDINATOR: Tim Manibusan
PRODUCTION EDITOR: Alice Mace Nakanishi
ILLUSTRATOR: Mary E. Flynn
PHOTO ASSISTANTS: Gregory Ligman and Kaeley Hammond
COVER PHOTOGRAPHY by Windborne Studios, Inc.
SUBJECTS PHOTOGRAPHY by Windborne Studios, Inc.;
INSTRUCTIONAL PHOTOGRAPHY by Estefany Gonzalez
of C&T Publishing, Inc., unless otherwise noted

Published by C&T Publishing, Inc., P.O. Box 1456, Lafayette, C 94549

Library of Congress Cataloging-in-Publication Data
Names: Berry, Ruth Ann, 1960- author.
Title: Stunning 3-D quilts simplified : create dimension with color, value &
geometric shapes / Ruth Ann Berry.
Other titles: Stunning three-D quilts simplified
Description: Lafayette, CA : C&T Publishing, 2020.
Identifiers: LCCN 2020006416 | ISBN 9781617459597 (trade paperback) |
ISBN 9781617459603 (ebook)
Subjects: LCSH: Quilting. | Quilting--Patterns.
Classification: LCC TT835 .B42754 2020 | DDC 746.46/041--dc23
LC record available at https://lccn.loc.gov/2020006416

Printed in the USA

10 9 8 7 6

Dedication

This book is dedicated to my husband, David, who quietly and patiently tolerates the "quilting thing" that he just doesn't understand.

Acknowledgments

Every creative spark requires a steady breeze to fan it into flame. Greg Barner is that whirlwind. He shapes brainstorms into reality and as Chief Stitch Master has pieced all the quilts for this book.

Contents

Introduction

I am captivated by any kind of artwork that is displayed on a flat surface but has the appearance of being a three-dimensional object.

To me, sidewalk chalk artists are the epitome of 3-D magicians. A little shading here, a little tweaking of perspective there, and a dimensional landscape appears on level pavement. Isn't it magic how the eye can create depth where there really isn't any? How fascinating that light and shadow applied with pencil, brush, or chalk can create dimension on a flat surface.

I have often wondered if a similar effect could be translated into fabric. Then I discovered isometric graph paper! Who knew?! If you draw an object on it, decide on a direction of an imaginary light source, and apply three values of shading … *Voilà!*—a dimensional object materializes.

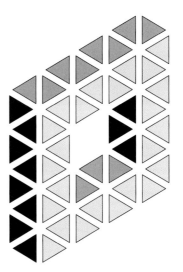

I noticed that 60° paper really is just vertical stacks of equilateral triangles. The triangles could easily be fabric in light, medium, and dark values to mimic the shading done with a pencil. The columns with triangles constructed vertically would eliminate any need for set-in seams, and the completed columns sewn together create the illusion of depth. Following this idea to conclusion, any gadget, gizmo, or doojigger you dare to imagine can become a 3-D quilt. The sky's the limit!

Making a 3-D Quilt

Tools

You won't need any specialized tools for these 3-D quilts, just a 60° triangle ruler and other basic sewing supplies. Here's a list of the tools I used.

- Rotary cutter and mat
- 6″ × 24″ straight ruler
- 60° triangle ruler with one blunt point
- Scissors
- Pins
- Marking pencil
- Clothes pins or binder clips

60° RULER OPTIONS

You don't have to buy a new 60° triangle ruler if yours doesn't have a blunt tip. To use a ruler with a pointed tip, align the bottom of the fabric strip with the ruler mark that is ¼″ more than the width of the strip.

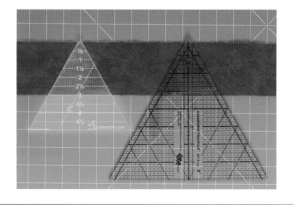

Selecting Fabric

To make one of these simplified 3-D quilts, choose blender, solid, or tone-on-tone fabrics in sets of three. Each box, beam, or square-nut element requires three fabrics—a light, a medium, and a dark. One option is to select fabrics of the same color in three values, as in *Echoes* (page 16). The fabrics within each colorway should graduate smoothly from light to dark but have enough contrast to be easily differentiated from each other.

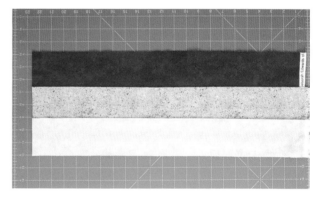

Another option is to choose three different colors for an element, still using a light, medium, and dark value but not necessarily the same color, as in *Soulmates* (page 44).

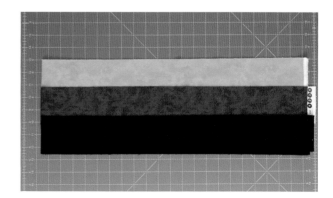

Using the Project Page

Each project page features a cutting chart that contains each fabric's color description, yardage requirement, and the number of triangles to cut from the strips.

Color	Width of strips and yardage	Triangles to cut from strips

Many of the projects offer more than one finished-size option based on the cut width of the strips. The patterns are easily sized up and down by changing the width of the strips. The strip width and finished size information is located at the top of the cutting chart. The yardage requirements and cutting instructions are provided for up to four different size options. These 3-D quilts are all constructed in columns of triangles, so that no Y-seams are required

---

Making the Quilt

CUTTING TRIANGLES FROM STRIPS

1. From the project page, choose a finished size and note the width of the strips required.

2. In each fabric color, start by cutting a width-of-fabric strip as indicated in the chart.

3. Starting at the selvage end of the strip, use a blunt-pointed 60° ruler to subcut the strip into equilateral triangles. *Note: Do not cut the border fabric into triangles!* If you have a 60° ruler with a pointed tip, see 60° Ruler Options (page 8).

4. Continue to cut strips and subcut triangles until you have the required number of triangles.

 TIP: How Many Triangles Can You Get From a Strip?

Assuming your fabric has 40˝ of usable width, you should be able to cut the following 60° triangles:

- 3˝ strip: 18 triangles
- 3½˝ strip: 15 triangles
- 4˝ strip: 13 triangles
- 5˝ strip: 11 triangles

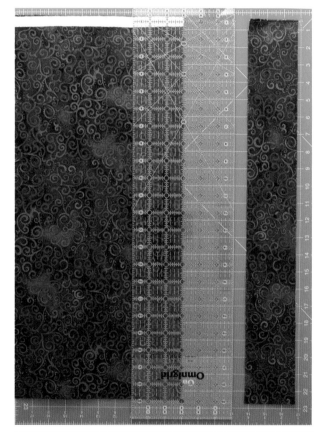

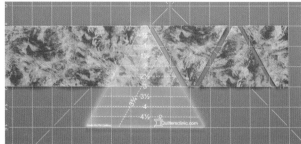

STACKING IN COLUMNS

1. Referring to the design chart, stack the triangles needed for each column in order from top to bottom, with the first triangle for the top of the column on the top of the stack.

2. Clip each stacked column together using a large project clip or clothespin.

Optional: Alternatively, you may choose to keep each color stacked separately and add triangles one at a time as you sew, marking off the design chart as you go.

SEWING COLUMNS

1. Sew each column, working from top to bottom. Use the triangle's blunt point as a "direction indicator" and match the orientation of each triangle to the design chart so the orientation of the triangles rotates from left to right. You can chain piece the triangles in pairs, then sets of 4, then sets of 8, and so on. Or if you find that confusing, you can also just add triangles one at a time working down the column.

2. If you're chain piecing, work down the column, sewing triangles together in pairs. Lay the first triangle in each pair on top of the next triangle, right sides together. Match the pointed tips. Using a ¼˝ seam allowance, sew the seam along the edge opposite the pointed tips.

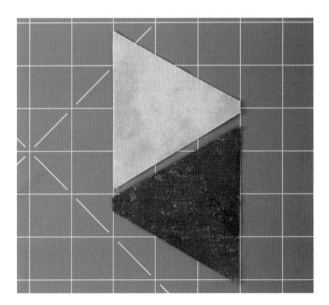

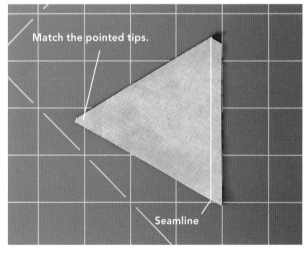

Match the pointed tips.

Seamline

3. Press the seams of the pairs open. Press the remaining seams open after the column is constructed. Don't trim off the "tails."

4. If you're chain piecing, sew the pairs into sets of 4, then sets of 8, and so on.

5. Use the pressed out "tails" to line up the pairs.

JOINING COLUMNS TOGETHER

Attach the columns together, working from left to right across the design chart. Use the pressed-out points to match each column to the next.

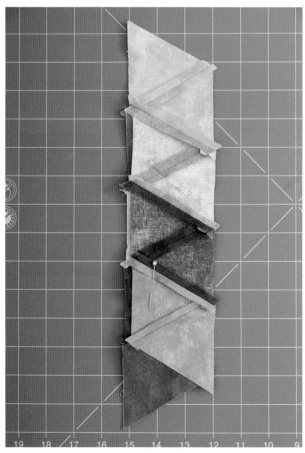

TIP: Alternate Sewing Direction

To avoid a curved result, alternate sewing direction with each new column, stitching from top to bottom, then bottom to top.

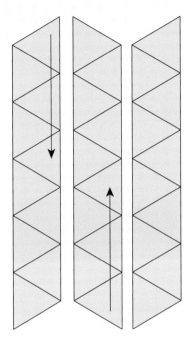

TRIMMING TO SQUARE

Trim the top and bottom edges of the quilt to square. Leave ¼˝ seam allowance.

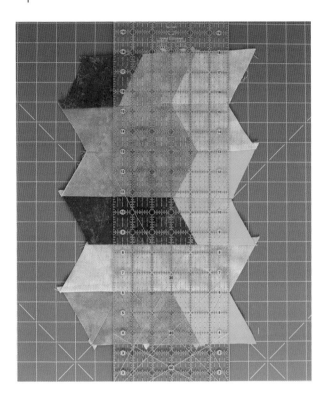

ADDING BORDERS

I usually add a simple border in the same fabric and strip width as the background fabric. This gives the design the appearance of "floating" on the background. I have listed the border yardage requirements separately from the background in the project charts so you can choose whatever fabric you wish. To add borders, measure the length of the side of the quilt to be bordered. Cut and piece a border strip to that length. Match the center of the border strip to the center of the quilt edge and pin in place. Pin the strip to the quilt edge, working from the center outward in both directions. Stitch in place.

FINISHING

Finish and bind using your preferred technique.

 TIP: Create a Row-Minder

One of the challenges of building a row-based (or column-based) quilt is keeping track of where you are in the pattern. Create a simple row-minder using a piece of paper or a semi-opaque plastic report cover, tape, and a paper clip or project clip. Cut the paper or report cover into 4 pieces: 2 rectangles 2″ × 11″ and 2 rectangles ¼″ × 4¼″. Place the 2 larger rectangles side by side with exactly a ¼″ space between them. Tape the smaller rectangles across the top and bottom of the larger pieces to create a ¼″ "window." Use a paper clip or project clip to hold the row-minder in place on your pattern.

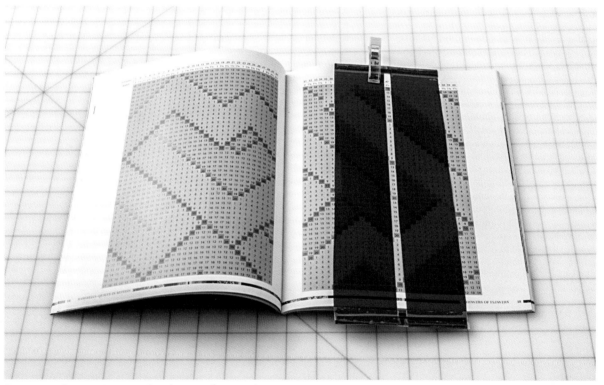

A row-minder in use on my book *Bargello—Quilts in Motion*

Photo by Diane Pedersen of C&T Publishing

PROJECTS

Echoes

Finished quilts: 50½″ × 69″ • 70½″ × 96½″

Designed by Ruth Ann Berry, pieced and quilted by Greg Barner, 2018

Weekend getaways are a great opportunity to doodle in a sketchbook. *Echoes* was drawn while I was wrapped in a blanket by the fireplace in a lovely vacation rental after a day of cross-country skiing with my friends in Michigan's Upper Peninsula. The name refers to the "bent-beam" elements in the drawing that "echo" one another by being the upside down and reverse of each other.

MATERIALS AND CUTTING

Start by cutting a strip in the width required for your quilt, then cut it into triangles (page 10). Continue to cut strips and triangles until you get the required number of triangles.

| Fabrics | Yardage requirements and width of strips | | Number of triangles |
	50½″ × 69″ quilt: Cut 3″ strips.	70½″ × 96½″ quilt: Cut 4″ strips.	
Light green	¼ yard	½ yard	37
Medium green	¼ yard	⅓ yard	26
Dark green	¼ yard	½ yard	30
Light blue	¼ yard	½ yard	37
Medium blue	¼ yard	½ yard	34
Dark blue	¼ yard	⅓ yard	22
Light aqua	¼ yard	½ yard	36
Medium aqua	¼ yard	⅓ yard	22
Dark aqua	¼ yard	½ yard	36
Light purple	¼ yard	½ yard	36
Medium purple	¼ yard	½ yard	32
Dark purple	¼ yard	⅓ yard	26
Light yellow	¼ yard	½ yard	29
Medium yellow	⅓ yard	⅝ yard	40
Dark yellow	⅓ yard	⅝ yard	46
Light pink	¼ yard	½ yard	29
Medium pink	⅓ yard	⅝ yard	46
Dark pink	⅓ yard	⅝ yard	40
Background	1¼ yards	1¾ yards	206
Border	¾ yard Cut 7 strips 3″ × WOF.*	1⅛ yards Cut 9 strips 4″ × WOF.	
Backing	3⅜ yards	6 yards	
Batting	58″ × 78″	78″ × 104″	

* WOF = width of fabric

Construction

See Making a 3-D Quilt (pages 11–13) for complete instructions on sewing the columns of triangles and assembling the quilt.

SEW THE COLUMNS

1. Start at the top left with a background triangle with the blunt point oriented toward the right and another background triangle with the blunt point oriented toward the left. To continue the first column, *add triangles in this order:*

  3 more background triangles

  1 light green

  5 dark green

  1 light pink

  10 dark pink

  1 background

  1 light pink

  7 dark pink

  1 light purple

  8 dark purple

  5 background

Following the *Echoes* design chart (page 19), alternate the left/right orientation of the triangles as you add them.

2. Complete the remaining columns in the same manner.

QUILT ASSEMBLY

1. Sew the columns together.

2. Trim the top and bottom of the quilt to square as described in Trimming to Square (page 13).

BORDERS

See Adding Borders (page 13). Before you cut the borders, measure your pieced quilt top and adjust the following sizes to match your quilt.

1. For the 50½˝ × 69˝ quilt, make 2 side borders 3˝ × 64˝ and top and bottom borders 3˝ × 50½˝. For the 70½˝ × 96½˝ quilt, make 2 side borders 4˝ × 89½˝ and top and bottom borders 4˝ × 70½˝.

2. Add the side borders to the quilt, then add the top and bottom borders.

Alternate Color Inspiration

Echoes design chart

Color Junction

Finished quilt: 70½″ × 100½″

Designed and quilted by Ruth Ann Berry, pieced by Greg Barner, 2018

Some people see Y's when they look at this classic design. I originally called it Corners, because that's what I see. But Greg said it needed a fancier name, so I looked for a synonym in the thesaurus. Junction was the closest thing to a fancy name for corners I could come up with. The beauty of this quilt is that it features a repeating pattern, so the quilt really can be any size you want. Just stop sewing when it's big enough or continue the design if you want more quilt.

MATERIALS AND CUTTING

Start by cutting a strip in the width required for your quilt, then cut it into triangles (page 10). Continue to cut strips and triangles until you get the required number of triangles.

Fabrics	Yardage requirements and width of strips	Number of triangles
	70½″ × 100½″ quilt: Cut 3″ strips.	
Light green	¾ yard	138
Medium green	¾ yard	122
Dark green	¾ yard	138
Light blue	¾ yard	132
Medium blue	¾ yard	138
Dark blue	¾ yard	122
Light red	¾ yard	132
Medium red	¾ yard	137
Dark red	¾ yard	121
Light yellow	¾ yard	140
Medium yellow	¾ yard	121
Dark yellow	¾ yard	137
Black	1 yard	164
Border	1 yard Cut 10 strips 3″ × WOF.	
Batting	78″ × 108″	
Backing	6⅛ yards	

* WOF = width of fabric

Continued on next page ⟶

Construction

See Making a 3-D Quilt (pages 11–13) for complete instructions on sewing the columns of triangles and assembling the quilt.

SEW THE COLUMNS

1. Start at the top with a black triangle with the blunt point oriented toward the right and a light yellow triangle oriented toward the left. To continue the first column, *add triangles in this order:*

2 dark yellow triangles

1 black

2 light blue

2 medium blue

1 light green

2 dark green

1 black

2 light red

2 medium red

1 light yellow

2 dark yellow

1 black

2 light blue

2 medium blue

1 light green

2 dark green

1 black

2 light red

2 medium red

1 light yellow

Color Junction **21**

2 dark yellow	2 light red	1 light green	Following the *Color Junction* design chart (next page), alternate the left/right orientation of the triangles as you add them.
1 black	2 medium red	2 dark green	
2 light blue	1 light yellow	1 black	
2 medium blue	2 dark yellow	2 light red	
1 light green	1 black	2 medium red	**2.** Complete the remaining columns in the same manner.
2 dark green	2 light blue	1 light yellow	
1 black	2 medium blue	1 black	

QUILT ASSEMBLY

1. Sew the columns together.

2. Trim the top and bottom of the quilt to square as described in Trimming to Square (page 13).

BORDERS

See Adding Borders (page 13). Before you cut the borders, measure your pieced quilt top and adjust the following sizes to match your quilt.

1. Make 2 side borders 3″ × 95½″ and top and bottom borders 3″ × 70½″.

2. Add the side borders to the quilt, then add the top and bottom borders.

Alternate Color Inspiration

Color Junction design chart

Reverie

Finished quilts: 50½″ × 73½″ • 70½″ × 102½″

Designed by Ruth Ann Berry, pieced and quilted by Greg Barner, 2018

Drawing and quilting are relaxation for the frazzled mind. They are good use of restful down-time. We stayed at a friend's house when we exhibited at the Chicago Quilt Show. They're wonderful hosts and there was plenty of after-show contemplation time to doodle the drawing that became *Reverie.*

MATERIALS AND CUTTING

Start by cutting a strip in the width required for your quilt, then cut it into triangles (page 10). Continue to cut strips and triangles until you get the required number of triangles.

Fabrics	Yardage requirements and width of strips		Number of triangles
	50½″ × 73½″ quilt: Cut 3″ strips.	70½″ × 102½″ quilt: Cut 4″ strips.	
Light green	⅓ yard	⅔ yard	53
Medium green	½ yard	1 yard	84
Dark green	⅓ yard	⅔ yard	45
Light red	¼ yard	½ yard	28
Medium red	¼ yard	½ yard	27
Dark red	⅓ yard	⅔ yard	48
Light blue	½ yard	⅔ yard	62
Medium blue	½ yard	¾ yard	72
Dark blue	⅓ yard	⅔ yard	47
Light yellow	¼ yard	½ yard	30
Medium yellow	¼ yard	⅓ yard	24
Dark yellow	⅓ yard	⅔ yard	46
Background	1½ yards	2⅔ yards	298
Border	¾ yard Cut 7 strips 3″ × WOF.*	1⅛ yards Cut 9 strips 4″ × WOF.	
Backing	3⅜ yards	6¼ yards	
Batting	58″ × 81″	78″ × 110″	

* WOF = width of fabric

Construction

See Making a 3-D Quilt (pages 11–13) for complete instructions on sewing the columns of triangles and assembling the quilt.

SEW THE COLUMNS

1. Start at the top left with a background triangle with the blunt point oriented toward the right and an additional background triangle oriented toward the left. To continue the first column, *add triangles in this order:*

3 more background triangles

1 light red

14 dark red

9 background

1 light blue

12 dark blue

6 background

Following the *Reverie* design chart (page 27), alternate the left/right orientation of the triangles as you add them.

2. Complete the remaining columns in the same manner.

QUILT ASSEMBLY

1. Sew the columns together.

2. Trim the top and bottom of the quilt to square as described in Trimming to Square (page 13).

BORDERS

See Adding Borders (page 13). Before you cut the borders, measure your pieced quilt top and adjust the following sizes to match your quilt.

1. For the 50½˝ × 73½˝ quilt, make 2 side borders 3˝ × 68½˝ and top and bottom borders 3˝ × 50½˝. For the 70½˝ × 102½˝ quilt, make 2 side borders 4˝ × 95½˝ and top and bottom borders 4˝ × 70½˝.

2. Add the side borders to the quilt, then add the top and bottom borders.

Alternate Color Inspiration

1 2 3 4 5 6 7 8 9 10 11 12 13 14 15 16 17 18

Reverie design chart

Chain Links

Finished quilts: 55½″ × 82″ • 77½″ × 114½″

Designed by Ruth Ann Berry, pieced by Greg Barner, quilted by Angie Taylor, 2018

Fabrics: Toscana Collection from Creator's Club program for Northcott Fabrics

The name *Chain Links* is descriptive of the eleven "links" in the drawing. I wanted the drawing to look like a twisted section of chain.

MATERIALS AND CUTTING

Start by cutting a strip in the width required for your quilt, then cut it into triangles (page 10). Continue to cut strips and triangles until you get the required number of triangles.

Fabrics	Yardage requirements and width of strips		Number of triangles
	55½″ × 82″ quilt: Cut 3″ strips.	77½″ × 114½″ quilt: Cut 4″ strips.	
Light green	½ yard	¾ yard	66
Medium green	½ yard	1 yard	79
Dark green	¼ yard	½ yard	35
Light blue	¼ yard	⅓ yard	24
Medium blue	⅓ yard	⅝ yard	50
Dark blue	⅓ yard	⅝ yard	52
Light purple	½ yard	¾ yard	67
Medium purple	½ yard	⅔ yard	60
Dark purple	⅓ yard	½ yard	39
Light yellow	½ yard	⅔ yard	64
Medium yellow	⅓ yard	⅝ yard	41
Dark yellow	½ yard	⅔ yard	62
Background	2¼ yards	4 yards	441
Border	¾ yard Cut 8 strips 3″ × WOF.*	1¼ yard Cut 10 strips 4″ × WOF.	
Backing	5⅛ yards	7¼ yards	
Batting	63″ × 90″	85″ × 122″	

* WOF = width of fabric

Construction

See Making a 3-D Quilt (pages 11–13) for complete instructions on sewing the columns of triangles and assembling the quilt.

SEW THE COLUMNS

1. Start at the top left with a background triangle with the blunt point oriented toward the left and an additional background triangle oriented to the right. To continue the first column, *add triangles in this order:*

> 10 more background triangles
>
> 1 light green
>
> 2 dark green
>
> 19 background
>
> 1 light blue
>
> 16 dark blue
>
> 3 background

Following the *Chain Links* design chart (page 31), alternate the left/right orientation of the triangles as you add them.

2. Complete the remaining columns in the same manner.

QUILT ASSEMBLY

1. Sew the columns together.

2. Trim the top and bottom of the quilt to square as described in Trimming to Square (page 13).

BORDERS

See Adding Borders (page 13). Before you cut the borders, measure your pieced quilt top and adjust the following sizes to match your quilt.

1. For the 55½″ × 82″ quilt, make 2 side borders 3″ × 77″ and top and bottom borders 3″ × 55½″. For the 77½″ × 114½″ quilt, make 2 side borders 4″ × 107½″ and top and bottom borders 4″ × 77½″.

2. Add the side borders to the quilt, then add the top and bottom borders.

Alternate Color Inspiration

Chain Links design chart

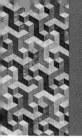

Treble

Finished quilt: 68″ × 94½″

Designed and quilted by Ruth Ann Berry, pieced by Greg Barner, 2018

The title *Treble* refers to the three-pronged nature of the drawing. It made me think of the treble hooks on a fishing lure. *Treble* features a repeating pattern that allows for flexibility in creating a smaller or larger quilt, lengthwise by reducing or increasing the number of triangles per column or widthwise by reducing or increasing the number of columns.

MATERIALS AND CUTTING

Start by cutting a strip in the width required for your quilt, then cut it into triangles (page 10). Continue to cut strips and triangles until you get the required number of triangles.

Fabrics	Yardage requirements and width of strips	Number of triangles
	68″ × 94½″ quilt: Cut 3″ strips.	
Light green	1 yard	150
Medium green	1 yard	152
Dark green	1 yard	148
Light blue	1 yard	150
Medium blue	1 yard	146
Dark blue	1 yard	152
Light purple	1 yard	146
Medium purple	1 yard	146
Dark purple	1 yard	148
Light yellow	1 yard	148
Medium yellow	1 yard	150
Dark yellow	1 yard	146
Backing	5⅞ yards	
Batting	76″ × 102″	

Continued on next page ⟶

Construction

See Making a 3-D Quilt (pages 11–13) for complete instructions on sewing the columns of triangles and assembling the quilt.

SEW THE COLUMNS

1. Start at the top left with a light purple triangle with the blunt point oriented toward the right and a medium purple triangle oriented toward the left. To continue the first column, *add triangles in this order:*

1 more medium purple triangle

1 light yellow

2 dark yellow

1 light blue

2 medium blue

2 light green

4 medium green

1 light green

2 dark green

2 light purple

6 dark purple

2 light green

2 dark green

1 light yellow

4 medium yellow

2 light purple

2 medium purple

1 light blue

2 dark blue

1 light blue

2 medium blue

1 light green

2 dark green

1 light blue

2 medium blue

2 light yellow

4 medium yellow

1 light yellow

2 dark yellow

2 light blue

4 dark blue

Following the *Treble* design chart (next page), alternate the left/right orientation of the triangles as you add them.

2. Complete the remaining columns in the same manner.

QUILT ASSEMBLY

1. Sew the columns together.

2. Trim the top and bottom of the quilt to square as described in Trimming to Square (page 13).

Alternate Color Inspiration

1 2 3 4 5 6 7 8 9 10 11 12 13 14 15 16 17 18 19 20 21 22 23 24 25 26 27

Treble design chart

Treble

Stormy

Finished quilts: 48″ × 63″ • 57½″ × 76″ • 67″ × 88½″

Designed by Ruth Ann Berry, pieced and quilted by Greg Barner, 2018

This drawing didn't turn out as planned. The look I was going for was one element crisscrossing over and then behind another element; but when I got done, it looked to me more like a lightning bolt, so I changed the color scheme and called it *Stormy.*

MATERIALS AND CUTTING

Start by cutting a strip in the width required for your quilt, then cut it into triangles (page 10). Continue to cut strips and triangles until you get the required number of triangles.

Fabrics	Yardage requirements and width of strips			Number of triangles
	48″ × 63″ quilt: Cut 3″ strips.	57½″ × 76″ quilt: Cut 3½″ strips.	67″ × 88½″ quilt: Cut 4″ strips.	
Light yellow	¾ yard	1 yard	1¼ yards	124
Medium yellow	⅓ yard	½ yard	⅔ yard	52
Dark yellow	½ yard	⅔ yard	⅔ yard	64
Light aqua	¼ yard	¼ yard	⅓ yard	19
Medium aqua	½ yard	½ yard	⅔ yard	55
Dark aqua	½ yard	½ yard	⅔ yard	56
Background	1¾ yards	2¼ yards	3 yards	327
Border	¾ yard Cut 6 strips 3″ × WOF.*	⅞ yard Cut 8 strips 3½″ × WOF.	1¼ yards Cut 9 strips 4″ × WOF.	
Backing	3¼ yards	4⅞ yards	5½ yards	
Batting	56″ × 71″	65″ × 84″	75″ × 96″	

* WOF = width of fabric

Construction

See Making a 3-D Quilt (pages 11–13) for complete instructions on sewing the columns of triangles and assembling the quilt.

SEW THE COLUMNS

1. Start at the top left with a background triangle with the blunt point oriented toward the right and another background triangle oriented toward the left. To continue the first column, *add triangles in this order:*

9 more background triangles

1 light yellow

2 dark yellow

13 background

1 light yellow

2 dark yellow

11 background

Following the *Stormy* design chart (page 39), alternate the left/right orientation of the triangles as you add them.

2. Complete the remaining columns in the same manner.

QUILT ASSEMBLY

1. Sew the columns together.

2. Trim the top and bottom of the quilt to square as described in Trimming to Square (page 13).

BORDERS

See Adding Borders (page 13). Before you cut the borders, measure your pieced quilt top and adjust the following sizes to match your quilt.

1. For the 48″ × 63″ quilt, make 2 side borders 3″ × 58″ and top and bottom borders 3″ × 48″.
For the 57½″ × 76″ quilt, make 2 side borders 3½″ × 70″ and top and bottom borders 3½″ × 57½″.
For the 67″ × 88½″ quilt, make 2 side borders 4″ × 81½″ and top and bottom borders 4″ × 67″.

2. Add the side borders to the quilt, then add the top and bottom borders.

Alternate Color Inspiration

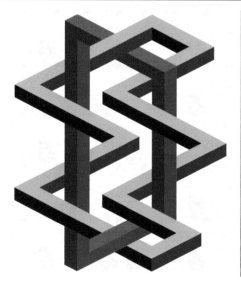  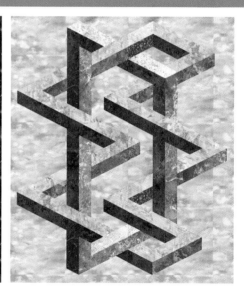

1 2 3 4 5 6 7 8 9 10 11 12 13 14 15 16 17

Stormy design chart

Harmony

Finished quilts: 60½″ × 72″ • 72½″ × 86″ • 84½″ × 100½″

Designed by Ruth Ann Berry, pieced and quilted by Greg Barner, 2018

Sometimes on an overnight drive to a quilt show, sleep deprivation and fatigue lead to silliness. A few late-night laugh sessions have been dedicated to developing a list of "approved quilt names." Since we love music, many of the names on the current list are music related.

MATERIALS AND CUTTING

Start by cutting a strip in the width required for your quilt, then cut it into triangles (page 10). Continue to cut strips and triangles until you get the required number of triangles.

Fabrics	Yardage requirements and width of strips			Number of triangles
	60½″ × 72″ quilt: Cut 3″ strips.	72½″ × 86″ quilt: Cut 3½″ strips.	84½″ × 100½″ quilt: Cut 4″ strips.	
Green	1 yard	1⅓ yards	1⅔ yards	166
Blue	1 yard	1¼ yards	1½ yards	153
Purple	1 yard	1¼ yards	1½ yards	145
Background	3 yards	3¾ yards	5 yards	570
Border	¾ yard Cut 7 strips 3″ × WOF.*	1 yard Cut 8 strips 3½″ × WOF.	1¼ yards Cut 10 strips 4″ × WOF.	
Backing	4 yards	5⅜ yards	7⅞ yards	
Batting	68″ × 80″	80″ × 94″	92″ × 108″	

* WOF = width of fabric

Construction

See Making a 3-D Quilt (pages 11–13) for complete instructions on sewing the columns of triangles and assembling the quilt.

SEW THE COLUMNS

1. Start at the top left with a background triangle with the blunt point oriented toward the right and another background triangle oriented toward the left. To continue the first column, *add triangles in this order:*

> 15 more background triangles
>
> 1 green
>
> 2 purple
>
> 7 background
>
> 1 green
>
> 2 purple
>
> 17 background

Following the *Harmony* design chart (page 43), alternate the left/right orientation of the triangles as you add them.

2. Complete the remaining columns in the same manner.

QUILT ASSEMBLY

1. Sew the columns together.

2. Trim the top and bottom of the quilt to square as described in Trimming to Square (page 13).

BORDERS

See Adding Borders (page 13). Before you cut the borders, measure your pieced quilt top and adjust the following sizes to match your quilt.

1. For the 60½″ × 72″ quilt, make 2 side borders 3″ × 67″ and top and bottom borders 3″ × 60½″.
For the 72½″ × 86″ quilt, make 2 side borders 3½″ × 80″ and top and bottom borders 3½″ × 72½″.
For the 84½″ × 100½″ quilt, make 2 side borders 4″ × 93½″ and top and bottom borders 4″ × 84½″.

2. Add the side borders to the quilt, then add the top and bottom borders.

Alternate Color Inspiration

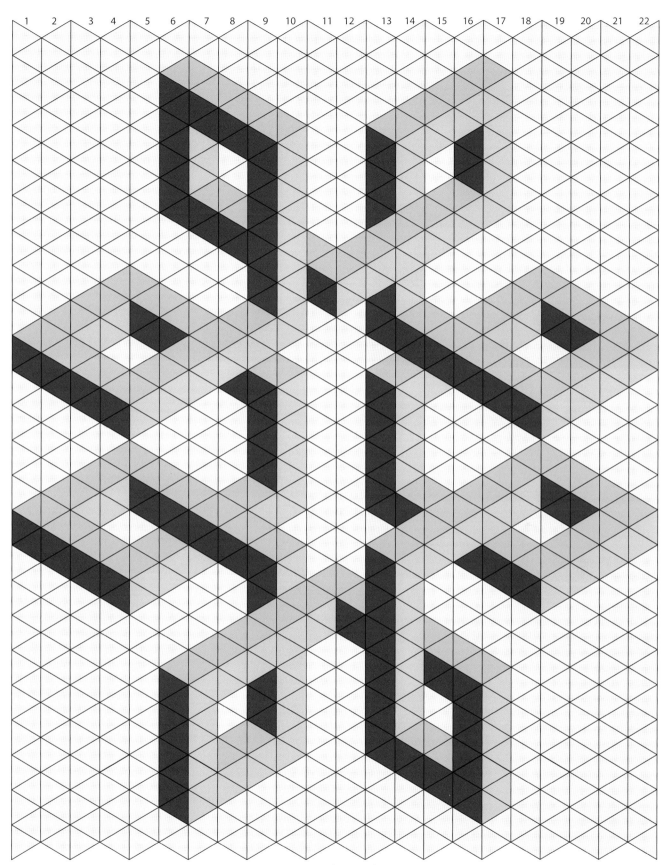

Harmony design chart

Soulmates

Finished quilts: 60½″ × 73½″ • 72½″ × 88″ • 84½″ × 102½″

Designed by Ruth Ann Berry, pieced and quilted by Greg Barner, 2018

The quilt title, *Soulmates*, is a reference to the two halves of the drawing that are the same but different, opposite but complementary, intertwined, heart to heart, and completing each other.

MATERIALS AND CUTTING

Start by cutting a strip in the width required for your quilt, then cut it into triangles (page 10). Continue to cut strips and triangles until you get the required number of triangles.

| Fabrics | Yardage requirements and width of strips | | | Number of triangles |
	60½″ × 73½″ quilt: Cut 3″ strips.	72½″ × 88″ quilt: Cut 3½″ strips.	84½″ × 102½″ quilt: Cut 4″ strips.	
Green	⅔ yard	1 yard	1¼ yards	112
Red	½ yard	¾ yard	1 yard	87
Black	⅔ yard	1 yard	1¼ yards	97
Yellow	⅔ yard	1 yard	1¼ yards	107
Aqua	⅔ yard	1 yard	1¼ yards	101
Purple	½ yard	¾ yard	1 yard	82
Background	2½ yards	3¼ yards	4¼ yards	470
Border	¾ yard Cut 7 strips 3″ × WOF.*	1 yard Cut 8 strips 3½″ × WOF.	1¼ yards Cut 10 strips 4″ × WOF.	
Backing	4 yards	5½ yards	7⅞ yards	
Batting	68″ × 81″	80″ × 96″	92″ × 110″	

* WOF = width of fabric

Construction

See Making a 3-D Quilt (pages 11–13) for complete instructions on sewing the columns of triangles and assembling the quilt.

SEW THE COLUMNS

1. Start at the top left with a background triangle with the blunt point oriented toward the right and another background triangle oriented toward the left. To continue the first column, *add triangles in this order:*

> 17 more background triangles
>
> 1 yellow
>
> 5 purple
>
> 1 green
>
> 2 black
>
> 8 purple
>
> 12 background

Following the *Soulmates* design chart (page 47), alternate the left/right orientation of the triangles as you add them.

2. Complete the remaining columns in the same manner.

QUILT ASSEMBLY

1. Sew the columns together.

2. Trim the top and bottom of the quilt to square as described in Trimming to Square (page 13).

BORDERS

See Adding Borders (page 13). Before you cut the borders, measure your pieced quilt top and adjust the following sizes to match your quilt.

1. For the 60½″ × 73½″ quilt, make 2 side borders 3″ × 68½″ and top and bottom borders 3″ × 60½″. For the 72½″ × 88″ quilt, make 2 side borders 3½″ × 82″ and top and bottom borders 3½″ × 72½″. For the 84½″ × 102½″ quilt, make 2 side borders 4″ × 95½″ and top and bottom borders 4″ × 84½″.

2. Add the side borders to the quilt, then add the top and bottom borders.

Alternate Color Inspiration

 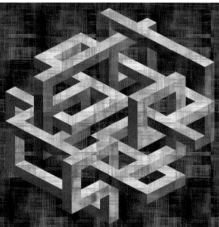 

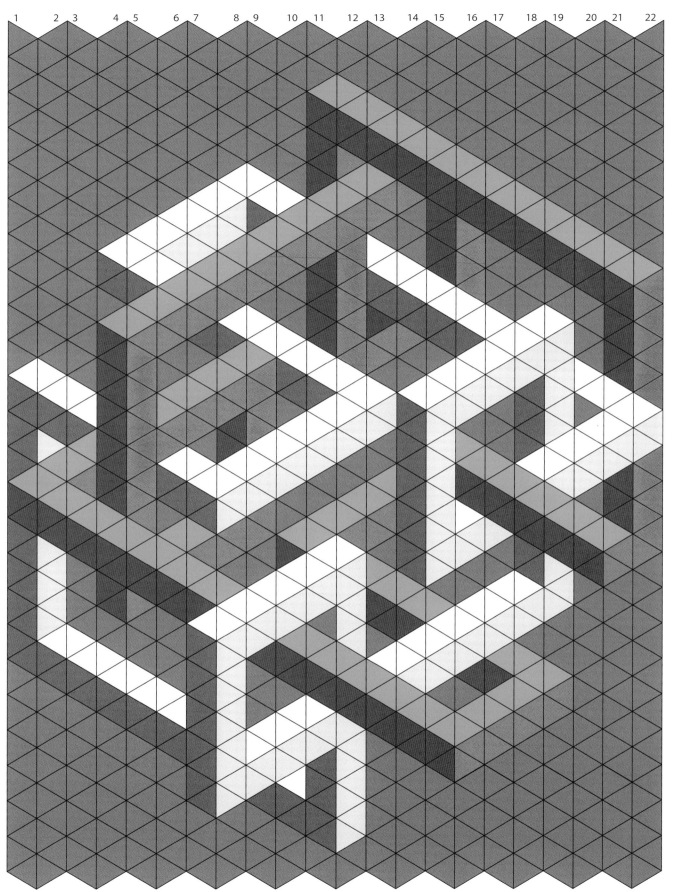

Soulmates design chart

Windigo

Finished quilts: 55½″ × 75″ • 66½″ × 89½″ • 77½″ × 104½″

Designed by Ruth Ann Berry, pieced and quilted by Greg Barner, 2017

Windigo is a place name in Isle Royale National Park, one of my favorite places to backpack. I think the word has its origins in Algonquian mythology. On Isle Royale, we usually get a boat taxi from Rock Harbor on the northeast end of the island down to Chippewa Harbor, then paddle and portage the inland lakes from there. The most inspirational place to sit with a sketchbook is the Wood Lake campground overlook facing Siskiwit Lake.

MATERIALS AND CUTTING

Start by cutting a strip in the width required for your quilt, then cut it into triangles (page 10). Continue to cut strips and triangles until you get the required number of triangles.

Fabrics	Yardage requirements and width of strips			Number of triangles
	55½″ × 75″ quilt: Cut 3″ strips.	66½″ × 89½″ quilt: Cut 3½″ strips.	77½″ × 104½″ quilt: Cut 4″ strips.	
Light green	½ yard	½ yard	⅔ yard	56
Medium green	⅔ yard	1 yard	1¼ yards	108
Dark green	⅔ yard	1 yard	1 yard	79
Light orange	½ yard	⅝ yard	1 yard	68
Medium orange	⅓ yard	½ yard	1 yard	51
Dark orange	⅔ yard	1 yard	1¼ yards	117
Light aqua	½ yard	⅝ yard	1 yard	74
Medium aqua	½ yard	¾ yard	1 yard	79
Dark aqua	⅔ yard	1 yard	1¼ yards	117
Background	1¼ yards	1¾ yards	2¼ yards	231
Border	¾ yard Cut 7 strips 3″ × WOF.*	1 yard Cut 8 strips 3½″ × WOF.	1¼ yards Cut 10 strips 4″ × WOF.	
Backing	4¾ yards	5½ yards	7¼ yards	
Batting	63″ × 83″	74″ × 97″	85″ × 112″	

* WOF = width of fabric

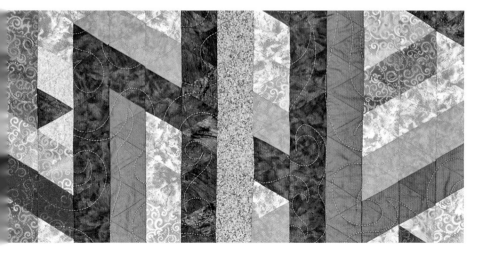

Construction

See Making a 3-D Quilt (pages 11–13) for complete instructions on sewing the columns of triangles and assembling the quilt.

SEW THE COLUMNS

1. Start at the top left with a background triangle with the blunt point oriented toward the left and another background triangle oriented toward the right. To continue the first column, *add triangles in this order:*

- 1 light aqua
- 10 dark aqua
- 1 background
- 1 light yellow
- 10 dark yellow
- 7 background
- 1 light green
- 14 dark green
- 2 background

Following the *Windigo* design chart (page 51), alternate the left/right orientation of the triangles as you add them.

2. Complete the remaining columns in the same manner.

QUILT ASSEMBLY

1. Sew the columns together.

2. Trim the top and bottom of the quilt to square as described in Trimming to Square (page 13).

BORDERS

See Adding Borders (page 13). Before you cut the borders, measure your pieced quilt top and adjust the following sizes to match your quilt.

1. For the 55½˝ × 75˝ quilt, make 2 side borders 3˝ × 70˝ and top and bottom borders 3˝ × 55½˝.
For the 66½˝ × 89½˝ quilt, make 2 side borders 3½˝ × 83½˝ and top and bottom borders 3½˝ × 66½˝.
For the 77½˝ × 104½˝ quilt, make 2 side borders 4˝ × 97½˝ and top and bottom borders 4˝ × 77½˝.

2. Add the side borders to the quilt, then add the top and bottom borders.

Alternate Color Inspiration

Windigo design chart

Floated

Finished quilts: 40½″ × 49″ • 48½″ × 58½″
56½″ × 68″ • 72½″ × 87½″

Designed by Ruth Ann Berry, pieced and quilted by Greg Barner, 2018

It seemed to me that the detached sections of the drawing had been "floated" on the background. It's a look that diverges from the continuous loop and the repeating pattern-style drawings. I think there are endless possibilities for expanding on the concept. So many ideas. So little time.

MATERIALS AND CUTTING

Start by cutting a strip in the width required for your quilt, then cut it into triangles (page 10). Continue to cut strips and triangles until you get the required number of triangles.

Fabrics	Yardage requirements and width of strips				Number of triangles
	40½″ × 49″ quilt: Cut 3″ strips.	48½″ × 58½″ quilt: Cut 3½″ strips.	56½″ × 68″ quilt: Cut 4″ strips.	72½″ × 87½″ quilt: Cut 5″ strips	
Light brown	½ yard	¾ yard	1 yard	1¼ yards	72
Medium brown	½ yard	¾ yard	1 yard	1¼ yards	72
Dark brown	½ yard	¾ yard	1 yard	1¼ yards	72
Background	1¼ yards	1⅔ yards	2 yards	3 yards	218
Border	½ yard Cut 5 strips 3″ × WOF.*	¾ yard Cut 6 strips 3½″ × WOF.	1 yard Cut 7 strips 4″ × WOF.	1¼ yards Cut 8 strips 5″ × WOF.	
Backing	2⅞ yards	3¼ yards	3¾ yards	5½ yards	
Batting	48″ × 57″	56″ × 66″	64″ × 76″	80″ × 95″	

* WOF = width of fabric

Construction

See Making a 3-D Quilt (pages 11–13) for complete instructions on sewing the columns of triangles and assembling the quilt.

SEW THE COLUMNS

1. Start at the top left with a background triangle with the blunt point oriented toward the left and another background triangle oriented toward the right. To continue the first column, *add triangles in this order:*

6 more background triangles

1 light brown

6 dark brown

1 background

1 light brown

6 dark brown

8 background

Following the *Floated* design chart (page 55), alternate the left/right orientation of the triangles as you add them.

2. Complete the remaining columns in the same manner.

QUILT ASSEMBLY

1. Sew the columns together.

2. Trim the top and bottom of the quilt to square as described in Trimming to Square (page 13).

BORDERS

See Adding Borders (page 13). Before you cut the borders, measure your pieced quilt top and adjust the following sizes to match your quilt.

1. For the 40½˝ × 49˝ quilt, make 2 side borders 3˝ × 44˝ and top and bottom borders 3˝ × 40½˝. For the 48½˝ × 58½˝ quilt, make 2 side borders 3½˝ × 52½˝ and top and bottom borders 3½˝ × 48½˝. For the 56½˝ × 68˝ quilt, make 2 side borders 4˝ × 61˝ and top and bottom borders 4˝ × 56½˝. For the 72½˝ × 87½˝ quilt, make 2 side borders 5˝ × 78½˝ and top and bottom borders 5˝ × 72½˝.

2. Add the side borders to the quilt, then add the top and bottom borders.

Alternate Color Inspiration

Floated design chart

Quaternity

Finished quilts: 55½″ × 64½″ • 66½″ × 77½″ • 77½″ × 90½″

Designed by Ruth Ann Berry, pieced and quilted by Greg Barner, 2018

In this quilt, there are four loops that form a continuous line. That makes it a "quartet" that loops for "eternity." I added two additional pieces to make the drawing more balanced and give it more color.

MATERIALS AND CUTTING

Start by cutting a strip in the width required for your quilt, then cut it into triangles (page 10). Continue to cut strips and triangles until you get the required number of triangles.

Fabrics	Yardage requirements and width of strips			Number of triangles
	55½″ × 64½″ quilt: Cut 3″ strips.	66½″ × 77½″ quilt: Cut 3½″ strips.	77½″ × 90½″ quilt: Cut 4″ strips.	
Light green	¼ yard	⅓ yard	⅓ yard	29
Medium green	½ yard	½ yard	⅔ yard	60
Dark green	⅓ yard	½ yard	½ yard	39
Light purple	¼ yard	½ yard	½ yard	34
Medium purple	½ yard	½ yard	⅔ yard	57
Dark purple	⅓ yard	½ yard	⅔ yard	48
Light orange	½ yard	¾ yard	1 yard	80
Medium orange	1 yard	1¼ yards	1½ yards	151
Dark orange	¾ yard	1 yard	1¼ yards	113
Background	1¼ yards	1⅔ yards	2¼ yards	229
Border	¾ yard Cut 6 strips 3″ × WOF.*	1 yard Cut 8 strips 3½″ × WOF.	1¼ yards Cut 9 strips 4″ × WOF.	
Backing	3⅝ yards	4⅞ yards	7¼ yards	
Batting	64″ × 72″	74″ × 85″	85″ × 98″	

* WOF = width of fabric

Construction

See Making a 3-D Quilt (pages 11–13) for complete instructions on sewing the columns of triangles and assembling the quilt.

SEW THE COLUMNS

1. Start at the top left with a background triangle with the blunt point oriented toward the left and another background triangle oriented toward the right. To continue the first column, *add triangles in this order:*

8 more background triangles

1 light purple

8 dark purple

5 background

8 dark purple

9 background

Following the *Quaternity* design chart (page 59), alternate the left/right orientation of the triangles as you add them.

2. Complete the remaining columns in the same manner.

QUILT ASSEMBLY

1. Sew the columns together.

2. Trim the top and bottom of the quilt to square as described in Trimming to Square (page 13).

BORDERS

See Adding Borders (page 13). Before you cut the borders, measure your pieced quilt top and adjust the following sizes to match your quilt.

1. For the 55½″ × 64½″ quilt, make 2 side borders 3″ × 59½″ and top and bottom borders 3″ × 55½″. For the 66½″ × 77½″ quilt, make 2 side borders 3½″ × 71½″ and top and bottom borders 3½″ × 66½″. For the 77½″ × 90½″ quilt, make 2 side borders 4″ × 83½″ and top and bottom borders 4″ × 77½″.

2. Add the side borders to the quilt, then add the top and bottom borders.

Alternate Color Inspiration

Quaternity design chart

Knots Table Runner

Finished table runner: 20½″ × 44″

Designed and quilted by Ruth Ann Berry, pieced by Greg Barner, 2019

Sometimes when I get an invitation to teach at quilt festivals, I get only a three-hour time slot. I needed a smaller project for the short classes so that we could get a larger percentage of it completed in class. *Knots* fits the bill. I thought the drawing had the look of a single-rope braid or a series of figure-eight knots.

MATERIALS AND CUTTING

Start by cutting a strip in the width required for your quilt, then cut it into triangles (page 10). Continue to cut strips and triangles until you get the required number of triangles.

Fabrics	Yardage requirements and width of strips	Number of triangles
	20½″ × 44″ table runner: Cut 3″ strips.	
Light blue	½ yard	84
Medium blue	⅓ yard	44
Dark blue	¼ yard	32
Background	⅔ yard	88
Backing	1⅝ yards	
Batting	28″ × 52″	

Construction

See Making a 3-D Quilt (pages 11–13) for complete instructions on sewing the columns of triangles and assembling the table runner.

SEW THE COLUMNS

1. Start at the top left with a background triangle with the blunt point oriented toward the right and another background triangle oriented toward the left. To continue the first column, *add triangles in this order:*

3 more back-ground triangles	1 light blue	3 background
1 light blue	2 dark blue	1 light blue
2 dark blue	3 background	2 dark blue
3 background	1 light blue	5 background
	2 dark blue	

Following the *Knots* design chart (page 62), alternate the left/right orientation of the triangles as you add them.

2. Complete the remaining columns in the same manner.

TABLE RUNNER ASSEMBLY

1. Sew the columns together.

2. Trim the top and bottom of the table runner to square as described in Trimming to Square (page 13).

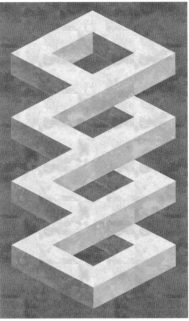

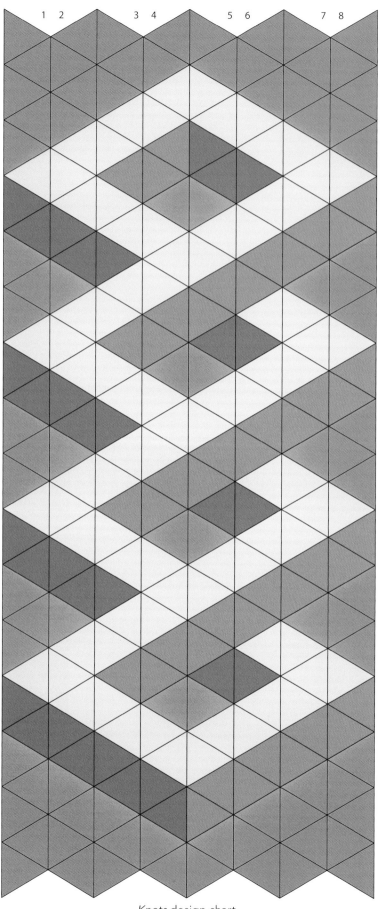

Knots design chart

About the Author

Ruth Ann Berry lives in rural northern Michigan where she owns a small-town quilt shop, The Quilter's Clinic, and writes books and patterns. Her clinic crew (sister, Nancy, and awesome employee, Angie) operate a busy online business and pack kits and patterns to ship all over the world.

She loves bright fabric, flowers, family gatherings, and outdoor adventure. She works part-time as a pharmacist and travels extensively for quilt guild presentations, trunk shows, and festivals.

Ruth Ann's focus is on drawing quilt patterns designed to create the impression of motion and depth, especially Bargello, 3-D geometric, and other three-dimensional styles.

She is the author of two previous books with C&T Publishing: *Bargello—Quilts in Motion* and *Braided Bargello Quilts*.

VISIT RUTH ANN ONLINE
AND FOLLOW ON SOCIAL MEDIA!

Website: quiltersclinic.com

Facebook: The Quilter's Clinic

ALSO BY RUTH ANN BERRY:

Photo by Mike Drilling, Windborne Photography Studio

CREATIVE SPARK
ONLINE LEARNING

Quilting courses to become an expert quilter...

From their studio to yours, Creative Spark instructors are teaching you how to create and become a master of your craft. So not only do you get a look inside their creative space, you also get to be a part of engaging courses that would typically be a one or multi-day workshop from the comfort of your home.

Creative Spark is not your one-size-fits-all online learning experience. We welcome you to be who you are, share, create, and belong.

Scan for a gift from us!

creativespark.ctpub.com